'I blush to say
what happened
next.'

GAIUS PETRONIUS ARBITER
Lived in the Roman Empire in the first century CE
Died *c.* 66 CE

Taken from J. P. Sullivan's translation of *The Satyricon*,
first published in 1965.

PETRONIUS IN PENGUIN CLASSICS
The Satyricon

PETRONIUS

Trimalchio's Feast

Translated by
J. P. Sullivan

PENGUIN BOOKS

PENGUIN CLASSICS

UK | USA | Canada | Ireland | Australia
India | New Zealand | South Africa

Penguin Books is part of the Penguin Random House group of companies
whose addresses can be found at global.penguinrandomhouse.com.

This selection published in Penguin Classics 2015
002

Translation copyright © J. P. Sullivan, 1965, 1969, 1974, 1977, 1986

The moral right of the translator has been asserted

Set in 9/12.4 pt Baskerville 10 Pro
Typeset by Jouve (UK), Milton Keynes
Printed in Great Britain by Clays Ltd, St Ives plc

A CIP catalogue record for this book is available from the British Library

ISBN: 978-0-141-39800-6

www.greenpenguin.co.uk

Penguin Random House is committed to a
sustainable future for our business, our readers
and our planet. This book is made from Forest
Stewardship Council® certified paper.

The next day but one finally arrived[, and that meant the prospect of a free dinner]. But we were so knocked about that we wanted to run rather than rest. We were mournfully discussing how to avoid the approaching storm, when one of Agamemnon's slaves broke in on our frantic debate.

'Here,' said he, 'don't you know who's your host today? It's Trimalchio – he's terribly elegant . . . He has a clock in the dining-room and a trumpeter all dressed up to tell him how much longer he's got to live.'

This made us forget all our troubles. We dressed carefully and told Giton, who was very kindly acting as our servant, to attend us at the baths.

We did not take our clothes off but began wandering around, or rather exchanging jokes while circulating among the little groups. Suddenly we saw a bald old man in a reddish shirt, playing ball with some long-haired boys. It was not so much the boys that made us watch, although they alone were worth the trouble, but the old gentleman himself. He was taking his exercise in slippers and throwing a green ball around. But he didn't pick it up if it touched the ground; instead there was a slave holding a bagful, and he supplied them to the players. We noticed other novelties. Two eunuchs stood around at different points: one of them carried a silver pissing bottle, the other counted the balls, not those flying from hand to hand according to the rules, but those that fell to the ground. We were still admiring these elegant arrangements when Menelaus hurried up to us.

'This is the man you'll be dining with,' he said. 'In fact, you are now watching the beginning of the dinner.'

No sooner had Menelaus spoken than Trimalchio snapped his fingers. At the signal the eunuch brought up the pissing bottle for him, while he went on playing. With the weight off his bladder, he demanded water for his hands, splashed a few drops on his fingers and wiped them on a boy's head.

It would take too long to pick out isolated incidents. Anyway, we entered the baths where we began sweating at once and we went immediately into the cold water. Trimalchio had been smothered in perfume and was already being rubbed down, not with linen towels, but with bath-robes of the finest wool. As this was going on, three masseurs sat drinking Falernian in front of him. Through quarrelling they spilled most of it and Trimalchio said they were drinking his health. Wrapped in thick scarlet felt he was put into a litter. Four couriers with lots of medals went in front, as well as a go-kart in which his favourite boy was riding – a wizened, bleary-eyed youngster, uglier than his master. As he was carried off, a musician with a tiny set of pipes took his place by Trimalchio's head and whispered a tune in his ear the whole way.

We followed on, choking with amazement by now, and arrived at the door with Agamemnon at our side. On the door-post a notice was fastened which read:

ANY SLAVE LEAVING THE HOUSE WITHOUT
HIS MASTER'S PERMISSION WILL RECEIVE
ONE HUNDRED LASHES

Just at the entrance stood the hall-porter, dressed in a green uniform with a belt of cherry red. He was shelling peas into a silver basin. Over the doorway hung – of all things – a golden cage from which a spotted magpie greeted visitors.

As I was gaping at all this, I almost fell over backwards and broke a leg. There, on the left as one entered, not far from the porter's cubbyhole, was a huge dog with a chain round its neck. It was painted on the wall and over it, in big capitals, was written:

BEWARE OF THE DOG

My colleagues laughed at me, but when I got my breath back I went on to examine the whole wall. There was a mural of a slave market, price-tags and all. Then Trimalchio himself, holding a wand of Mercury and being led into Rome by Minerva. After this a picture of how he learned accounting and, finally, how he became a steward. The painstaking artist had drawn it all in great detail with descriptions underneath. Just where the colonnade ended Mercury hauled him up by the chin and rushed him to a high platform. Fortune with her horn of plenty and the three Fates spinning their golden threads were there in attendance.

I also noticed in the colonnade a company of runners practising with their trainer. In one corner was a large cabinet, which served as a shrine for some silver statues of the

3

household deities with a marble figure of Venus and an impressive gold casket in which, they told me, the master's first beard was preserved.

I began asking the porter what were the pictures they had in the middle.

'The Iliad, the Odyssey,' he said, 'and the gladiatorial show given by Laenas.'

Time did not allow us to look at many things there . . . by now we had reached the dining-room, at the entrance to which sat a treasurer going over the accounts. There was one feature I particularly admired: on the door-posts were fixed rods and axes tapering off at their lowest point into something like the bronze beak of a ship. On it was the inscription:

PRESENTED TO C. POMPEIUS TRIMALCHIO
PRIEST OF THE AUGUSTAN COLLEGE
BY HIS STEWARD CINNAMUS

Beneath this same inscription a fixture with twin lamps dangled from the ceiling and two notices, one on each door-post. One of them, if my memory is correct, had written on it:

30 AND 31 DECEMBER
OUR GAIUS
IS OUT TO DINNER

The other displayed representations of the moon's phases and the seven heavenly bodies. Lucky and unlucky days were marked with different coloured studs.

Having had enough of these interesting things, we attempted to go in, but one of the slaves shouted: 'Right foot first!' Naturally we hesitated a moment in case one of us should cross the threshold the wrong way. But just as we were all stepping forward, a slave with his back bare flung himself at our feet and began pleading with us to get him off a flogging. He was in trouble for nothing very serious, he told us – the steward's clothes, hardly worth ten sesterces, had been stolen from him at the baths. Back went our feet, and we appealed to the steward, who was counting out gold pieces in the office, to let the man off.

He lifted his head haughtily: 'It is not so much the actual loss that annoys me,' he said, 'it's the wretch's carelessness. They were my dinner clothes he lost. A client had presented them to me on my birthday – genuine Tyrian purple, of course; however they had been laundered once. So what does it matter? He's all yours.'

We were very much obliged to him for this favour; and when we did enter the dining-room, that same slave whose cause we had pleaded ran up to us and, to our utter confusion, covered us with kisses and thanked us for our kindness.

'And what's more,' he said, 'you'll know right away who it is you have been so kind to. "The master's wine is the waiter's gift."'

Finally we took our places. Boys from Alexandria poured iced water over our hands. Others followed them and attended to our feet, removing any hangnails with great skill. But they were not quiet even during this troublesome operation: they sang away at their work. I wanted to find out if

5

the whole staff were singers, so I asked for a drink. In a flash a boy was there, singing in a shrill voice while he attended to me – and anyone else who was asked for something did the same. It was more like a musical comedy than a respectable dinner party.

Some extremely elegant hors d'oeuvres were served at this point – by now everyone had taken his place with the exception of Trimalchio, for whom, strangely enough, the place at the top was reserved. The dishes for the first course included an ass of Corinthian bronze with two panniers, white olives on one side and black on the other. Over the ass were two pieces of plate, with Trimalchio's name and the weight of the silver inscribed on the rims. There were some small iron frames shaped like bridges supporting dormice sprinkled with honey and poppy seed. There were steaming hot sausages too, on a silver gridiron with damsons and pomegranate seeds underneath.

We were in the middle of these elegant dishes when Trimalchio himself was carried in to the sound of music and set down on a pile of tightly stuffed cushions. The sight of him drew an astonished laugh from the guests. His cropped head stuck out from a scarlet coat; his neck was well muffled up and he had put round it a napkin with a broad purple stripe and tassels dangling here and there. On the little finger of his left hand he wore a heavy gilt ring and a smaller one on the last joint of the next finger. This I thought was solid gold, but actually it was studded with little iron stars. And to show off even more of his jewellery, he had his right arm bare and set off by a gold armlet and an ivory circlet fastened with a gleaming metal plate.

After picking his teeth with a silver toothpick, he began: 'My friends, I wasn't keen to come into the dining-room yet. But if I stayed away any more, I would have kept you back, so I've deprived myself of all my little pleasures for you. However, you'll allow me to finish my game.'

A boy was at his heels with a board of terebinth wood with glass squares, and I noticed the very last word in luxury – instead of white and black pieces he had gold and silver coins. While he was swearing away like a trooper over his game and we were still on the hors d'oeuvres, a tray was brought in with a basket on it. There sat a wooden hen, its wings spread round it the way hens are when they are broody. Two slaves hurried up and as the orchestra played a tune they began searching through the straw and dug out peahens' eggs, which they distributed to the guests.

Trimalchio turned to look at this little scene and said: 'My friends, I gave orders for that bird to sit on some peahens' eggs. I hope to goodness they are not starting to hatch. However, let's try them and see if they are still soft.'

We took up our spoons (weighing at least half a pound each) and cracked the eggs, which were made of rich pastry. To tell the truth, I nearly threw away my share, as the chicken seemed already formed. But I heard a guest who was an old hand say: 'There should be something good here.' So I searched the shell with my fingers and found the plumpest little figpecker, all covered with yolk and seasoned with pepper.

At this point Trimalchio became tired of his game and demanded that all the previous dishes be brought to him. He gave permission in a loud voice for any of us to have another glass of mead if we wanted it. Suddenly there was a crash from the orchestra and a troop of waiters – still singing – snatched away the hors d'oeuvres. However in the confusion one of the side-dishes happened to fall and a slave picked it up from the floor. Trimalchio noticed this, had the boy's ears boxed and told him to throw it down again. A cleaner came in with a broom and began to sweep up the silver plate along with the rest of the rubbish. Two long-haired Ethiopians followed him, carrying small skin bags like those used by the men who scatter the sand in the amphitheatre, and they poured wine over our hands – no one ever offered us water.

Our host was complimented on these elegant arrangements. 'Mars loves a fair fight,' he replied. 'That is why I gave orders for each guest to have his own table. At the same time these smelly slaves won't crowd so.'

Carefully sealed wine bottles were immediately brought, their necks labelled:

FALERNIAN
CONSUL OPIMIUS
ONE HUNDRED YEARS OLD

While we were examining the labels, Trimalchio clapped his hands and said with a sigh:

'Wine has a longer life than us poor folks. So let's wet our whistles. Wine is life. I'm giving you real Opimian. I didn't put out such good stuff yesterday, though the company was much better class.'

Naturally we drank and missed no opportunity of admiring his elegant hospitality. In the middle of this a slave brought in a silver skeleton, put together in such a way that its joints and backbone could be pulled out and twisted in all directions. After he had flung it about on the table once or twice, its flexible joints falling into various postures, Trimalchio recited:

> 'O woe, woe, man is only a dot:
> Hell drags us off and that is the lot;
> So let us live a little space,
> At least while we can feed our face.'

After our applause the next course was brought in. Actually it was not as grand as we expected, but it was so novel that everyone stared. It was a deep circular tray with the twelve signs of the Zodiac arranged round the edge. Over each of them the chef had placed some appropriate dainty suggested by the subject. Over Aries the Ram, chickpeas; over Taurus the Bull, a beefsteak; over the Heavenly Twins, testicles and kidneys; over Cancer the Crab, a garland; over Leo the Lion, an African fig; over Virgo the Virgin, a young sow's udder; over Libra the Scales, a balance with a cheesecake in one pan and a pastry in the other; over Scorpio, a sea scorpion; over Sagittarius the Archer, a sea bream with eyespots; over Capricorn, a lobster; over Aquarius the Water-Carrier, a goose; over Pisces the Fishes, two mullets. In the centre was a piece of grassy turf bearing a honeycomb. A young Egyptian slave carried around bread in a silver oven . . . and in a sickening voice he mangled a song from the show *The Asafoetida Man*.

As we started rather reluctantly on this inferior fare, Trimalchio said:

'Let's eat, if you don't mind. This is the sauce of all order.' As he spoke, four dancers hurtled forward in time to the music and removed the upper part of the great dish, revealing underneath plump fowls, sows' udders, and a hare with wings fixed to his middle to look like Pegasus. We also noticed four figures of Marsyas with little skin bottles, which let a peppery fish-sauce go running over some fish, which seemed to be swimming in a little channel. We all joined in the servants' applause and amid some laughter we helped ourselves to these quite exquisite things.

Trimalchio was every bit as happy as we were with this sort of trick: 'Carve 'er!' he cried. Up came the man with the carving knife and, with his hands moving in time to the orchestra, he sliced up the victuals like a charioteer battling to the sound of organ music. And still Trimalchio went on saying insistently: 'Carve 'er, Carver!'

I suspected this repetition was connected with some witticism, and I went so far as to ask the man on my left what it meant. He had watched this sort of game quite often and said:

'You see the fellow doing the carving – he's called Carver. So whenever he says "Carver!" he's calling out his name and his orders.'

I couldn't face any more food. Instead I turned to this man to find out as much as I could. I began pestering him for gossip and information – who was the woman running round the place?

'Trimalchio's wife,' he told me, 'Fortunata is her name and

she counts her money by the sackful. And before, before, what was she? You'll pardon me saying so, but you wouldn't of touched a bit of bread from her hand. Nowadays – and who knows how or why – she's in heaven, and she's absolutely everything to Trimalchio. In fact, if she tells him at high noon it's dark, he'll believe her. He doesn't know himself how much he's got, he's so loaded – but this bitch looks after everything; she's even in places you wouldn't think of. She's dry, sober and full of ideas – you see all that gold! – but she's got a rough tongue and she's a real magpie when she gets her feet up. If she likes you, she likes you – if she doesn't like you, she doesn't like you.

'The old boy himself now, he's got estates it'd take a kite to fly over – he's worth millions of millions. There's more silver plate lying in his porter's cubbyhole than any other man owns altogether. As for his servants – boy, oh boy! I honestly don't think there's one in ten knows his own master. In fact he could knock any of these smart boys into a cocked hat.

'And don't you think he buys anything, either. Everything is home-grown: wool, citrus, pepper. If you ask for hen's milk, you'll get it. In fact, there was a time when the wool he'd got wasn't good enough for him, so he brought some rams from Tarentum and banged them into his sheep. To get home-grown Attic honey, he ordered some bees from Athens – the Greek strain improved his own bees a bit at the same time.

'And here's something more – this last few days he wrote off for mushroom spores from India. Why, he hasn't a single mule that wasn't sired by a wild ass. You see all these cushions – every one of them has either purple or scarlet stuffing. There's happiness for you!

'But mind you, don't look down on the other freedmen here. They're dripping with the stuff. You see that man on the very bottom couch. At present he's got eight hundred thousand of his own. He started out with nothing. It's not long since he was humping wood on his own back. They say – I don't know myself, I've heard it – they say he stole a hobgoblin's cap and found its treasure. I don't begrudge anyone what god has given him. Besides, he can still feel his master's slap and wants to give himself a good time. For instance, the other day he put up a notice which said:

GAIUS POMPEIUS DIOGENES
IS MOVING TO HIS HOUSE AND
WILL LET THE ROOM OVER
HIS SHOP FROM 1 JULY

'Now that fellow in the freedman's place – look how well off he was once! I'm not blaming him – he had a million in his hands, but he slipped badly. I don't think he can call his hair his own. Yet I'd swear it wasn't his fault: there's not a better man alive. Some freedmen and crooks pocketed everything he had. One thing you can be sure of – you have partners and your pot never boils, and once things take a turn for the worse, friends get out from underneath. What a respectable business he had and look at him now! He was an undertaker. He used to eat like a king – boars roasted in their skins, elaborate pastry, braised game birds, as well as fish and hares. More wine was spilt under the table than another man keeps in his cellar. He wasn't a man, he was an absolute dream! When things were looking black, he didn't want his creditors to think he was bankrupt, so he put up notice of an auction like this:

GAIUS JULIUS PROCULUS
AUCTION OF SURPLUS STOCK'

Trimalchio interrupted these pleasant reminiscences. The dish had already been removed and the convivial guests had begun to concentrate on the drink and general conversation. Leaning on his elbow, Trimalchio said:

'Now you're supposed to be enjoying the wine. Fishes have to swim. I ask you, do you think I'm just content with that course you saw in the bottom of the dish? "Is this like the Ulysses you know?" Well then, we've got to display some culture at our dinner. My patron – God rest his bones! – wanted me to hold up my head in any company. There's nothing new to me, as that there dish proves. Look now, these here heavens, as there are twelve gods living in 'em, changes into that many shapes. First it becomes the Ram. So whoever is born under that sign has a lot of herds, a lot of wool, a hard head as well, a brassy front and a sharp horn. Most scholars are born under this sign, and most mutton-heads as well.'

We applauded the wit of our astrologer and he went on:

'Then the whole heavens turns into the little old Bull. So bullheaded folk are born then, and cow-herds and those who find their own feed. Under the Heavenly Twins on the other hand – pairs-in-hand, yokes of oxen, people with big ballocks and people who do it both ways. I was born under the Crab, so I have a lot of legs to stand on and a lot of property on land and sea, because the Crab takes both in his stride. And that's why I put nothing over him earlier, so as not to upset my horoscope. Under Leo are born greedy and bossy people. Under the Virgin, effeminates, runaways and candidates for the chain-gang. Under the Scales, butchers, perfume-sellers and anyone who weighs things up. Under Scorpio poisoners and murderers. Under Sagittarius are born cross-eyed people who look at the vegetables and take the bacon. Under Capricorn, people in trouble who sprout horns through their worries. Under the Water-Carrier, bartenders and jugheads. Under the Fishes, fish-fryers and people who spout in public.

'So the starry sky turns round like a millstone, always bringing some trouble, and men being born or dying.

'Now as for what you see in the middle, the piece of grass and on the grass the honeycomb, I don't do anything without a reason – it's Mother Earth in the middle, round like an egg, with all good things inside her like a honeycomb.'

'Oh, clever!' we all cried, raising our hands to the ceiling and swearing that Hipparchus and Aratus couldn't compete with *him*.

Then the servants came up and laid across the couches embroidered coverlets showing nets, hunters carrying broad spears, and all the paraphernalia of hunting. We were still wondering which way to look when a tremendous clamour arose outside the dining-room, and – surprise! – Spartan hounds began dashing everywhere, even round the table. Behind them came a great dish and on it lay a wild boar of the largest possible size, and, what is more, wearing a freedman's cap on its head. From its tusks dangled two baskets woven from palm leaves, one full of fresh Syrian dates, the other of dried Theban dates. Little piglets made of cake were all round as though at its dugs, suggesting it was a brood sow now being served. These were actually gifts to take home. Surprisingly the man who took his place to cut up the boar was not our old friend Carver but a huge bearded fellow, wearing leggings and a damask hunting coat. He pulled out a hunting knife and made a great stab at the boar's side and, as he struck, out flew a flock of thrushes. But there were fowlers all ready with their limed reeds, who caught them as soon as they began flying round the room.

Trimalchio gave orders for each guest to have his own bird, then added:

'And have a look at the delicious acorns our pig in the wood has been eating.'

Young slaves promptly went to the baskets and gave the guests their share of the two kinds of date.

As this was going on, I kept quiet, turning over a lot of ideas as to why the boar had come in with a freedman's cap on it. After working through all sorts of wild fancies, I ventured to put to my experienced neighbour the question I was racking my brains with. He of course replied:

'Even the man waiting on you could explain this obvious point – it's not puzzling at all, it's quite simple. The boar here was pressed into service for the last course yesterday, but the guests let it go. So today it returns to the feast as a freedman.'

I damned my own stupidity and asked no more questions in case I looked like someone who had never dined in decent company.

As we were talking, a handsome youth with a garland of vine-leaves and ivy round his head, pretending to be Bacchus the Reveller, then Bacchus the Deliverer and Bacchus the Inspirer, carried grapes round in a basket, all the time giving us a recital of his master's lyrics in a high-pitched voice. At the sound, Trimalchio called out, 'Dionysus, now be Bacchus the Liberat . . .'

The lad pulled the freedman's cap off the boar and stuck it on his head. Then Trimalchio commented:

'Now you won't deny my claim to be the liberated sort.' We applauded his joke and kissed the boy hard as he went round.

After this course Trimalchio got up and went to the toilet. Free of his domineering presence, we began to help ourselves to more drinks. Dama started off by calling for a cup of the grape.

'The day's nothin',' he said. 'It's night 'fore y'can turn around. So the best thing's get out of bed and go straight to dinner. Lovely cold weather we've had too. M'bath hardly thawed me out. Still, a hot drink's as good as an overcoat. I've been throwin' it back neat, and you can see I'm tight – the wine's gone to m'head.'

Seleucus took up the ball in the conversation:

'Me now,' he said, 'I don't have a bath every day. It's like getting rubbed with fuller's earth, havin' a bath. The water bites into you, and your heart begins to melt. But when I've knocked back a hot glass of wine and honey, "Go fuck yourself," I say to the cold weather. Mind you, I couldn't have a bath – I was at a funeral today. Poor old Chrysanthus has just given up the ghost – nice man he was! It was only the other day he stopped me in the street. I still seem to hear his voice. Dear, dear! We're just so many walking bags of wind. We're worse than flies – at least they have got some strength in them, but we're no more than empty bubbles.

'And yet he had been on an extremely strict diet? For five days he didn't take a drop of water or a crumb of bread into his mouth. But he's gone to join the majority. The doctors finished him – well, hard luck, more like. After all, a doctor is just to put your mind at rest. Still, he got a good send-off – he had a bier, and all beautifully draped. His mourners – several of his slaves were left their freedom – did him proud, even though his widow was a bit mean with her tears. And yet he had been extremely good to her! But women as a sex are real vultures. It's no good doing them a favour, you might as well throw it down a well. An old passion is just an ulcer.'

He was being a bore and Phileros said loudly:

'Let's think of the living. He's got what he deserved. He lived an honest life and he died an honest death. What has he got to complain about? He started out in life with just a penny and he was ready to pick up less than that from a muck-heap, even if he had to use his teeth. So whatever he put a finger to swelled up like a honeycomb. I honestly think he left a solid hundred thousand and he had the lot in hard cash. But I'll be honest about it, since I'm a bit of a cynic: he had a foul mouth and too much lip. He wasn't a man, he was just trouble.

'Now his brother was a brave lad, a real friend to his friends, always ready with a helping hand or a decent meal.

'Chrysanthus had bad luck at first, but the first vintage set him on his feet. He fixed his own price when he sold the wine. And what properly kept his head above water was a legacy he came in for, when he pocketed more than was left to him. And the blockhead, when he had a quarrel with his brother, cut him out of his will in favour of some sod we've never heard of. You're leaving a lot behind when you leave your own flesh and blood. But he kept listening to his slaves and they really fixed him. It's never right to believe all you're told, especially for a businessman. But it's true he enjoyed himself while he lived. You got it, you keep it. He was certainly Fortune's favourite – lead turned to gold in his hand. Mind you, it's easy when everything runs smoothly.

'And how old do you think he was? Seventy or more! But he was hard as a horn and carried his age well. His hair was black as a raven's wing. I knew the man for ages and ages and he was still an old lecher. I honestly don't think he left the dog alone. What's more, he liked little boys – he could turn his hand to anything. Well, I don't blame him – after all, he couldn't take anything else with him.'

This was Phileros, then Ganymedes said:

'You're all talking about things that don't concern heaven or earth. Meanwhile, no one gives a damn the way we're hit by the corn situation. Honest to god, I couldn't get hold of a mouthful of bread today. And look how there's still no rain. It's been absolute starvation for a whole year now. To hell with the food officers! They're in with the bakers – "You be nice to me and I'll be nice to you." So the little man suffers, while those grinders of the poor never stop celebrating. Oh, if only we still had the sort of men I found here when I first arrived from Asia. Like lions they were. That was the life! Come one, come all! If plain flour was inferior to the very finest, they'd thrash those bogeymen till they thought God Almighty was after them.

'I remember Safinius – he used to live by the old arch then; I was a boy at the time. He wasn't a man, he was all pepper. He used to scorch the ground wherever he went. But he was dead straight – don't let him down and he wouldn't let you down. You'd be ready to play *morra* with him in the dark. But on the city council, how he used to wade into some of them – no beating about the bush, straight from the shoulder! And when he was in court, his voice got louder and louder like a trumpet. He never sweated or spat – I think he'd been through the oven all right. And very affable he was when you met him, calling everyone by name just like one of us. Naturally at the time corn was dirt cheap. You could buy a penny loaf that two of you couldn't get through. Today – I've seen bigger bull's-eyes.

'Ah me! It's getting worse every day. This place is going down like a calf's tail. But why do we have a third-rate food officer who wouldn't lose a penny to save our lives? He sits at home laughing and rakes in more money a day than anyone else's whole fortune. I happen to know he's just made a thousand in gold. But if we had any balls at all, he wouldn't be feeling so pleased with himself. People today are lions at home and foxes outside.

'Take me. I've already sold the rags off my back for food and if this shortage continues I'll be selling my bit of a house. What's going to happen to this place if neither god nor man will help us? As I hope to go home tonight, I'm sure all this is heaven's doing.

'Nobody believes in heaven, see, nobody fasts, nobody gives a damn for the Almighty. No, people only bow their heads to count their money. In the old days high-class ladies used to climb up the hill barefoot, their hair loose and their hearts pure, and ask God for rain. And he'd send it down in bucketfuls right away – it was then or never – and everyone went home like drowned rats. Since we've given up religion the gods nowadays keep their feet wrapped up in wool. The fields just lie . . .'

'Please, please,' broke in Echion the rag-merchant, 'be a bit more cheerful. "First it's one thing, then another," as the yokel said when he lost his spotted pig. What we haven't got today, we'll have tomorrow. That's the way life goes. Believe me, you couldn't name a better country, if it had the people. As things are, I admit, it's having a hard time, but it isn't the only place. We mustn't be soft. The sky don't get no nearer wherever you are. If you were somewhere else, you'd be talking about the pigs walking round ready-roasted back here.

'And another thing, we'll be having a holiday with a three-day show that's the best ever – and not just a hack troupe of gladiators but freedmen for the most part. My old friend Titus has a big heart and a hot head. Maybe this, maybe that, but something at all events. I'm a close friend of his and he's no way wishy-washy. He'll give us cold steel, no quarter and the slaughterhouse right in the middle where all the stands can see it. And he's got the wherewithal – he was left thirty million when his poor father died. Even if he spent four hundred thousand, his pocket won't feel it and he'll go down in history. He's got some real desperadoes already, and a woman who fights in a chariot, and Glyco's steward who was caught having fun with his mistress. You'll see quite a quarrel in the crowd between jealous husbands and romantic lovers. But that half-pint Glyco threw his steward to the lions, which is just giving himself away. How is it the servant's fault when he's forced into it? It's that old pisspot who really deserves to be tossed by a bull. But if you can't beat the ass you beat the saddle. But how did Glyco imagine that poisonous daughter of Hermogenes would ever turn out well? The old man could cut the claws off a flying kite, and a snake don't hatch old rope. Glyco – well, Glyco's got his. He's branded for as long as he lives and only the grave will get rid of it. But everyone pays for their sins.

'But I can almost smell the dinner Mammaea is going to give us – two denarii apiece for me and the family. If he really does it, he'll make off with all Norbanus's votes, I tell you he'll win at a canter. After all, what good has Norbanus done us? He put on some half-pint gladiators, so done in already that they'd have dropped if you blew at them. I've seen beast fighters give a better performance. As for the horsemen killed, he got them off a lamp – they ran round like cocks in a backyard. One was just a cart-horse, the other couldn't stand up, and the reserve was just one corpse instead of another – he was practically hamstrung. One boy did have a bit of spirit – he was in Thracian armour, and even he didn't show any initiative. In fact, they were all flogged afterwards, there were so many shouts of "Give 'em what for!" from the crowd. Pure cowards, that's all.

21

'"Well, I've put on a show for you," he says. "And I'm clapping you," says I. "Reckon it up – I'm giving more than I got. So we're quits."'

'Hey, Agamemnon! I suppose you're saying "What is that bore going on and on about?" It's because a good talker like you don't talk. You're a cut above us, and so you laugh at what us poor people say. We all know you're off your head with all that reading. But never mind! Will I get you some day to come down to my place in the country and have a look at our little cottage? We'll find something to eat – a chicken, some eggs. It'll be nice, even though the weather this year has ruined everything. Anyway, we'll find enough to fill our bellies.

'And by now my little lad is growing up to be a student of yours. He can divide by four already. If he stays well, you'll have him ready to do anything for you. In his spare time, he won't take his head out of his exercise book. He's clever and there's good stuff in him, even if he is crazy about birds. Only yesterday I killed his three goldfinches and told him a weasel ate them. But he's found some other silly hobbies, and he's having a fine time painting. Still, he's already well ahead with his Greek, and he's starting to take to his Latin, though his tutor is too pleased with himself and unreliable. He's well-educated but doesn't want to work. There is another one too, not so trained but he is conscientious – he teaches the boy more than he knows himself. In fact, he even makes a habit of coming around on holidays, and whatever you give him, he's happy.

'Anyway, I've just bought the boy some law books, as I want him to pick up some legal training for home use.

There's a living in that sort of thing. He's done enough dab-
bling in poetry and such like. If he objects, I've decided he'll
learn a trade – barber, auctioneer, or at least a barrister –
something he can't lose till he dies. Well, yesterday I gave it
to him straight: "Believe me, my lad, any studying you do
will be for your own good. You see Phileros the lawyer – if
he hadn't studied, he'd be starving today. It's not so long
since he was humping round stuff to sell on his back. Now
he can even look Norbanus in the face. An education is an
investment, and a proper profession never goes dead on
you."'

This was the sort of chatter flying round when Trimalchio
came in, dabbed his forehead and washed his hands in
perfume. There was a very short pause, then he said:

'Excuse me, dear people, my inside has not been answer-
ing the call for several days now. The doctors are puzzled.
But some pomegranate rind and resin in vinegar has done
me good. But I hope now it will be back on its good behav-
iour. Otherwise my stomach rumbles like a bull. So if any
of you wants to go out, there's no need for him to be embarrassed. None of us was born solid. I think there's nothing so
tormenting as holding yourself in. This is the one thing even
God Almighty can't object to. Yes, laugh, Fortunata, but you
generally keep me up all night with this sort of thing.

'Anyway, I don't object to people doing what suits them
even in the middle of dinner – and the doctors forbid
you to hold yourself in. Even if it's a longer business, everything is there just outside – water, bowls, and all the other
little comforts. Believe me, if the wind goes to your brain it
starts flooding your whole body too. I've known a lot of

people die from this because they wouldn't be honest with themselves.'

We thanked him for being so generous and considerate and promptly proceeded to bury our amusement in our glasses. Up to this point we'd not realized we were only half-way up the hill, as you might say.

The orchestra played, the tables were cleared, and then three white pigs were brought into the dining-room, all decked out in muzzles and bells. The first, the master of ceremonies announced, was two years old, the second three, and the third six. I was under the impression that some acrobats were on their way in and the pigs were going to do some tricks, the way they do in street shows. But Trimalchio dispelled this impression by asking:

'Which of these would you like for the next course? Any clodhopper can do you a barnyard cock or a stew and trifles like that, but my cooks are used to boiling whole calves.'

He immediately sent for the chef and without waiting for us to choose he told him to kill the oldest pig.

He then said to the man in a loud voice:

'Which division are you from?'

When he replied he was from number forty, Trimalchio asked:

'Were you bought or were you born here?'

'Neither,' said the chef, 'I was left to you in Pansa's will.'

'Well, then,' said Trimalchio, 'see you serve it up carefully – otherwise I'll have you thrown into the messengers' division.'

So the chef, duly reminded of his master's magnificence, went back to his kitchen, the next course leading the way.

Trimalchio looked round at us with a gentle smile: 'If you

don't like the wine, I'll have it changed. It is up to you to do it justice. I don't buy it, thank heaven. In fact, whatever wine really tickles your palate this evening, it comes from an estate of mine which as yet I haven't seen. It's said to join my estates at Tarracina and Tarentum. What I'd like to do now is add Sicily to my little bit of land, so that when I want to go to Africa, I could sail there without leaving my own property.

'But tell me, Agamemnon, what was your debate about today? Even though I don't go in for the law, still I've picked up enough education for home consumption. And don't you think I turn my nose up at studying, because I have two libraries, one Greek, one Latin. So tell us, just as a favour, what was the topic of your debate?'

Agamemnon was just beginning, 'A poor man and a rich man were enemies . . .' when Trimalchio said: 'What's a poor man?' 'Oh, witty!' said Agamemnon, and then told us about some fictitious case or other. Like lightning Trimalchio said: 'If this happened, it's not a fictitious case – if it didn't happen, then it's nothing at all.'

We greeted this witticism and several more like it with the greatest enthusiasm.

'Tell me, my dear Agamemnon,' continued Trimalchio, 'do you remember the twelve labours of Hercules and the story of Ulysses – how the Cyclops tore out his eye with his thumb. I used to read about them in Homer, when I was a boy. In fact, I actually saw with my own eyes the Sybil at Cumae dangling in a bottle, and when the children asked her in Greek: "What do you want, Sybil?" she used to answer: "I want to die."'

25

He was still droning on when a server carrying the massive pig was put on the table. We started to express our amazement at this speed and swear that not even an ordinary rooster could be cooked so quickly, the more so as the pig seemed far larger than it had appeared before. Trimalchio looked closer and closer at it, and then shouted:

'What's this? Isn't this pig gutted? I'm damn certain it isn't. Call the chef in here, go on, call him!'

The downcast chef stood by the table and said he'd forgotten it.

'What, you forgot!' shouted Trimalchio. 'You'd think he'd only left out the pepper and cumin. Strip him!'

In a second the chef was stripped and standing miserably between two guards. But everyone began pleading for him:

'It does tend to happen,' they said, 'do let him off, please. If he does it any more, none of us will stand up for him again.'

Personally, given my tough and ruthless temperament, I couldn't contain myself. I leaned over and whispered in Agamemnon's ear:

'This has surely got to be the worst slave in the world. Could anyone forget to clean a pig? I damn well wouldn't let him off if he forgot to clean a fish.'

But not Trimalchio. His face relaxed into a smile.

'Well,' he said, 'since you have such a bad memory, gut it in front of us.'

The chef recovered his shirt, took up a knife and with a nervous hand cut open the pig's belly left and right. Suddenly, as the slits widened with the pressure, out poured sausages and blood-puddings.

The staff applauded this trick and gave a concerted cheer – 'Hurray for Gaius!' The chef of course was rewarded with a drink and a silver crown, and was also given a drinking cup on a tray of Corinthian bronze. Seeing Agamemnon staring hard at this cup, Trimalchio remarked:

'I'm the only person in the world with genuine Corinthian.'

I was expecting him with his usual conceit to claim that all his plate came from Corinth. But he was not as bad as that.

'Perhaps you're wondering,' he went on, 'how I'm the only one with genuine Corinthian dishes. The simple reason is that the manufacturer I buy from is named Corinth – but what can be Corinthian, if you don't have a Corinth to get it from?

'You mustn't take me for a fool: I know very well where Corinthian metalwork first came from. When Troy was captured that crafty snake Hannibal piled all the bronze, silver and gold statues into one heap and set them on fire, and they were all melted to a bronze alloy. The metalworkers took this solid mass and made plates, dishes, and statuettes out of it. That is how Corinthian plate was born, not really one thing or another, but everything in one. You won't mind my saying so, but I prefer glass – that's got no taste at all. If only it didn't break, I'd prefer it to gold, but it's cheap stuff the way it is.

'Mind you, there was a craftsman once who made a glass bowl that didn't break. So he got an audience with the Emperor, taking his present with him . . . Then he made Caesar hand it back to him and dropped it on the floor. The Emperor couldn't have been more shaken. The man picked the bowl off the ground – it had been dinted like a bronze dish – took a hammer from his pocket and easily got the bowl as good as new. After this performance he thought he'd be in high heaven, especially when the Emperor said to him:

' "Is there anyone else who knows this process for making glass?"

'But now see what happens. When the man said no, the Emperor had his head cut off, the reason being that if it was made public, gold would have been as cheap as muck.

'Now I'm very keen on silver. I have some three-gallon bumpers more or less . . . how Cassandra killed her sons, and the boys are lying there dead – very lifelike. I have a bowl my patron left to me with Daedalus shutting Niobe in the Trojan Horse. What's more, I have the fights of Hermeros and Petraites on some cups – all good and heavy. No, I wouldn't sell my know-how at any price.'

While he was talking, a young slave dropped a cup. Trimalchio looked in his direction.

'Get out and hang yourself,' he said, 'you're utterly useless.' Immediately the boy's lips trembled and he begged Trimalchio's pardon.

'What are you asking me for?' snapped his master, 'as though I was the trouble! I'm just asking you not to let yourself be such a useless fool.'

In the end however, as a favour to us, he let him off and the boy ran round the table to celebrate . . . and shouted, 'Out with the water – in with the wine!'

We all showed our appreciation of his amusing wit – especially Agamemnon, who knew how to angle for further invitations. But our admiration went to Trimalchio's head. He drank with even greater cheerfulness and was very nearly drunk by now.

'Doesn't anyone want my dear Fortunata to dance?' he said. 'Honestly, no one dances the *Cordax* better.'

Then he stuck his hands up over his forehead and gave us a personal imitation of the actor Syrus, while all the staff sang in chorus:

'Madeia, Perimadeia.'

In fact, he would have taken the floor, if Fortunata had not whispered in his ear. She must have told him, I suppose, that such low fooling did not suit his dignity. But you never saw anyone so changeable – one minute he would be frightened of Fortunata and the next minute he would be back in character again.

What really interrupted his coarse insistence on dancing was his accountant, who sounded as though he was reading out a copy of the Gazette:

'26 July: Births on the estate at Cumae: male 30, female 40. Wheat threshed and stored: 500,000 pecks. Oxen broken in: 500.

'On the same date: the slave Mithridates crucified for insulting the guardian spirit of our dear Gaius.

'On the same date: Deposits to the strong-room (no further investment possible): 10,000,000 sesterces.

'On the same date: a fire broke out on the estate at Pompeii beginning at the house of Nasta the bailiff.'

'What!' said Trimalchio. 'When was an estate bought for me at Pompeii?'

'Last year,' said the accountant, 'so it hasn't yet come on the books.'

Trimalchio flared up:

'If any land is bought for me and I don't hear of it within six months, I refuse to have it entered on the books.'

The official edicts were read out and the wills of certain gamekeepers. In specific codicils they said they were leaving Trimalchio nothing. Then the names of some bailiffs; the divorce of a freed-woman, the wife of a watchman, on the grounds of adultery with a bath-attendant; the demotion of a hall-porter to a job at Baiae; the prosecution of a steward; and the result of an action between some bedroom attendants.

Finally the acrobats arrived. One was a silly idiot who stood there holding a ladder and made his boy climb up the rungs, give us a song and dance at the top, then jump through blazing hoops, and hold up a large wine-jar with his teeth.

Only Trimalchio was impressed by all this: art wasn't appreciated, he considered, but if there were two things in the world he really liked to watch, they were acrobats and horn-players. All the other shows were not worth a damn.

'As a matter of fact,' he said, 'once I even bought some comic-actors, but I preferred them putting on Atellan farces, and I told my conductor to keep his songs Latin.'

Just as he was saying this, the boy tumbled down on Trimalchio's couch. Everyone screamed, the guests as well as the servants – not because they were worried over such an awful person (they would happily have watched his neck

being broken) but because it would have been a poor ending
to the party if they had to offer their condolences for a com-
parative stranger. Trimalchio himself groaned heavily and
leaned over his arm as though it were hurt. Doctors raced to
the scene, but practically the first one there was Fortunata,
hair flying and cup in hand, telling the world what a poor
unfortunate thing she was. As for the boy who had fallen,
he was already crawling round our feet, begging for mercy.
I had a very uneasy feeling that his pleadings might be the
prelude to some funny surprise ending, as I still remembered
the chef who had forgotten to gut his pig. So I began looking round the dining-room for some machine to appear out
of the wall, especially after a servant was beaten for using
white instead of purple wool to bandage his master's
bruised arm.

Nor were my suspicions far out, because instead of
punishment, there came an official announcement from Trimalchio that the boy was free, so that no one could say that
such a great figure had been injured by a slave.

We all applauded his action and started a desultory conversation about how uncertain life was.

'Well,' says Trimalchio, 'an occasion like this mustn't pass
without a suitable record.' He immediately called for his
notebook, and without much mental exertion he came out
with:

> 'What comes next you never know,
> Lady Luck runs the show,
>   So pass the Falernian, lad.'

This epigram brought the conversation round to poetry and for quite a time the first place among poets was given to Mopsus of Thrace until Trimalchio said:

'Tell me, professor, how would you compare Cicero and Publilius? I think Cicero was the better orator, but Publilius the better man. Now could there be anything finer than this:

> Down luxury's maw, Mars' walls now wilt.
> Your palate pens peacocks in plumage of gilt:
> These Babylon birds are plumped under lock
> With the guinea hen and the capon cock.
> That long-legged paragon, winged castanet,
> Summer's lingering lease and winter's regret –
> Even the stork, poor wandering guest,
> Is put in your pot and makes that his nest.
> Why are Indian pearls so dear in your sight?
> So your sluttish wife, draped in the diver's delight,
> May open her legs on her lover's divan?
> What use are green emeralds, glass ruin of man,
> Or carbuncles from Carthage with fire in their flint?
> Unless to let goodness gleam out in their glint.
> Is it right for a bride to be clad in a cloud
> Or wearing a wisp show off bare to the crowd?

'Well now, whose profession do we think is most difficult after literature? I think doctors and bankers. A doctor has to know what people have in their insides and what causes a fever – even though I do hate them terribly the way they put me on a diet of duck. A banker has to spot the brass under the silver. Well, among dumb animals the hardest worked are cattle and sheep. It's thanks to cattle we have bread to eat, and it's thanks to sheep and their wool that we're well dressed. It's a low trick the way we eat mutton and wear woollens. Bees, now, I think are heavenly creatures – they spew honey, though people suppose they get it from heaven. But at the same time they sting, because where there's sweet you'll find bitter there too.'

He was still putting the philosophers out of work when tickets were brought round in a cup and the boy whose job it was read out the presents. '*Rich man's prison* – a silver jug. *Pillow* – a piece of neck came up. *Old man's wit and a sour stick* – dry salt biscuits came up and an apple on a stick. *Lick and spit* got a whip and a knife. *Flies and a fly-trap* was raisins and Attic honey. *Dinner-clothes and city-suit* got a slice of meat and a notebook. *Head and foot* produced a hare and a slipper. *Lights and letters* got a lamprey and some peas.' We laughed for ages. There were hundreds of things like this but they've slipped my mind now.

Ascyltus, with his usual lack of restraint, found everything extremely funny, lifting up his hands and laughing till the tears came. Eventually one of Trimalchio's freedman friends flared up at him.

'You with the sheep's eyes,' he said, 'what's so funny? Isn't our host elegant enough for you? You're better off, I suppose, and used to a bigger dinner. Holy guardian here preserve me! If I was sitting by him, I'd stop his bleating! A fine pippin he is to be laughing at other people! Some fly-by-night from god knows where – not worth his own piss. In fact, if I pissed round him, he wouldn't know where to turn.

'By god, it takes a lot to make me boil, but if you're too

soft, worms like this only come to the top. Look at him laughing! What's he got to laugh at? Did his father pay cash for him? You're a Roman knight, are you? Well, my father was a king.

'"*Why are you only a freedman?*" did you say? Because I put myself into slavery. I wanted to be a Roman citizen, not a subject with taxes to pay. And today, I hope no one can laugh at the way I live. I'm a man among men, and I walk with my head up. I don't owe anybody a penny – there's never been a court-order out for me. No one's said "*Pay up*" to me in the street.

'I've bought a bit of land and some tiny pieces of plate. I've twenty bellies to feed, as well as a dog. I bought my old woman's freedom so nobody could wipe his dirty hands on *her* hair. Four thousand I paid for myself. I was elected to the Augustan College and it cost me nothing. I hope when I die I won't have to blush in my coffin.

'But you now, you're such a busybody you don't look behind you. You see a louse on somebody else, but not the fleas on your own back. You're the only one who finds us funny. Look at the professor now – he's an older man than you and we get along with him. But you're still wet from your mother's milk and not up to your ABC yet. Just a crackpot – you're like a piece of wash-leather in soak, softer but no better! You're grander than us – well, have two dinners and two suppers! I'd rather have my good name than any amount of money. When all's said and done, who's ever asked me for money twice? For forty years I slaved but nobody ever knew if I was a slave or a free man. I came to this colony when I was a lad with long hair – the town hall hadn't been built then. But I worked hard to please my master – there was a real gentleman, with more in his little finger-nail than there is in your whole body. And I had people in the house who tried to trip me up one way or another, but still – thanks be to his guardian spirit! – I kept my head above water. These are the prizes in life: being born free is as easy as all get-out. Now what are you gawping at, like a goat in a vetch-field?'

At this remark, Giton, who was waiting on me, could not suppress his laughter and let out a filthy guffaw, which did not pass unnoticed by Ascyltus' opponent. He turned his abuse on the boy.

'So!' he said. 'You're amused too, are you, you curly-headed onion? A merry Saturnalia to you! Is it December, I'd like to know? When did *you* pay your liberation tax? . . . Look, he doesn't know what to do, the gallow's bird, the crow's meat.

'God's curse on you, and your master too, for not keeping you under control! As sure as I get my bellyful, it's only because of Trimalchio that I don't take it out of you here and now. He's a freedman like myself. We're doing all right, but those good-for-nothings, well – . It's easy to see, like master, like man. I can hardly hold myself back, and I'm not naturally hot-headed – but once I start, I don't give a penny for my own mother.

'All right! I'll see you when we get outside, you rat, you excrescence. I'll knock your master into a cocked hat before I'm an inch taller or shorter. And I won't let you off either, by heaven, even if you scream down God Almighty. Your cheap curls and your no-good master won't be much use to you then – I'll see to that. I'll get my teeth into you all right. Either I'm much mistaken about myself or you won't be laughing at us behind your golden beard. Athena's curse on you and the man who first made you such a forward brat.

'I didn't learn no geometry or criticism and such silly rubbish, but I can read the letters on a notice board and I can do my percentages in metal, weights, and money. In fact, if you like, we'll have a bet. Come on, here's my cash. Now you'll see how your father wasted his money, even though you do know how to make a speech.

'Try this:

> Something we all have.
> Long I come, broad I come. What am I?

'I'll give you it: something we all have that runs and doesn't move from its place: something we all have that grows and gets smaller.

'You're running round in circles, you've had enough, like the mouse in the pisspot. So either keep quiet or keep out of the way of your betters – they don't even know you're alive – unless you think I care about your box-wood rings that you swiped from your girl-friend! Lord make me lucky! Let's go into town and borrow some money. You'll soon see they trust this iron one.

'Pah! a drownded fox makes a nice sight, I must say. As I hope to make my pile and die so famous that people swear by my dead body, I'll hound you to death. And he's a nice thing too, the one who taught you all these tricks – a mutton-head, not a master. We learned different. Our teacher used to say: "Are your things in order? Go straight home.

No looking around. And be polite to your elders." Nowadays it's all an absolute muck-heap. They turn out nobody worth a penny. I'm like you see me and I thank god for the way I was learnt.'

Ascyltus began to answer this abuse, but Trimalchio, highly amused by his friend's fluency, said:

'No slanging matches! Let's all have a nice time. And you, Hermeros, leave the young fellow alone. His blood's a bit hot – you should know better. In things like this, the one who gives in always comes off best. Besides, when you were just a chicken, it was cock-a-doodle too, and you had no more brains yourself. So let's start enjoying ourselves again, that'll be better, and let's watch the recitations from Homer.'

In came the troupe immediately and banged their shields with their spears. Trimalchio sat up on his cushion and while the reciters spouted their Greek lines at one another in their usual impudent way, he read aloud in Latin in a sing-song voice. After a while, he got silence and asked:

'Do you know which scene they were acting? Diomede and Ganymede were the two brothers. Their sister was Helen. Agamemnon carried her off and offered a hind to Diana in her place. So now Homer is describing how the Trojans and Tarentines fought each other. Agamemnon, of course, won and married off his daughter Iphigenia to Achilles. This drove Ajax insane, and in a moment or two he'll explain how it ended.'

As Trimalchio said this, the reciters gave a loud shout, the servants made a lane, and a calf was brought in on a two-hundred pound plate: it was boiled whole and wearing a helmet. Following it came Ajax, slashing at the calf with a drawn sword like a madman. After rhythmically cutting and slicing, he collected the pieces on the point and shared them among the surprised guests.

But we were not given long to admire these elegant turns, for all of a sudden, the coffered ceiling began rumbling and the whole dining-room shook. I leapt to my feet in panic, as I was afraid some acrobat was coming down through the roof. The other guests also looked up to see what strange visitation this announced. Would you believe it – the panels opened and suddenly an enormous hoop was let down, with gold crowns and alabaster jars of toilet cream hanging from it. While we were being told to accept these as presents, I looked at the table . . . Already there was a tray of cakes in position, the centre of which was occupied by a Priapus made of pastry, holding the usual things in his very adequate lap – all kinds of apples and grapes.

Greedily enough, we stretched out our hands to this display, and in a flash a fresh series of jokes restored the general gaiety. Every single cake and every single apple needed only the slightest touch for a cloud of saffron to start pouring out and the irritating vapour to come right in our faces.

Naturally we thought the dish must have some religious significance to be smothered in such an odour of sanctity, so we raised ourselves to a sitting position and cried:

'God save Augustus, the Father of his People!'

All the same, even after this show of respect, some of the guests were snatching the apples – especially me, because I didn't think I was pushing a generous enough share into Giton's pocket.

While all this was going on, three boys in brief white tunics came in. Two of them set down on the table the household deities, which had amulets round their necks; the other, carrying round a bowl of wine, kept shouting: 'God save all here!' . . .

Our host said that one of the gods was called Cobbler, the second Luck, and the third Lucre. There was also a golden image of Trimalchio himself, and as all the others were pressing their lips to it we felt too embarrassed not to do the same.

After we had all wished each other health and happiness, Trimalchio looked at Niceros and said:

'You used to be better company at a party. You're keeping very quiet nowadays: you don't say a word – I don't know why. Do me a favour to please me. Tell us about that adventure you had.'

Niceros was delighted by his friend's affable request and said:

'May I never make another penny if I'm not jumping for joy to see you in such form. Well, just for fun – though I'm worried about those schoolteachers there in case they laugh at me. That's up to them. I'll tell it all the same. Anyway, what do I care who laughs at me. It's better to be laughed at than laughed down.'

'*When thus he spake*,' he began this story:

'When I was still a slave, we were living down a narrow street – Gavilla owns the house now – and there as heaven would have it, I fell in love with the wife of Terentius the innkeeper.

'You all used to know Melissa from Tarentum, an absolute

peach to look at. But honest to god, it wasn't her body or just sex that made me care for her, it was more because she had such a nice nature. If I asked her for anything, it was never refused. If I had a penny or halfpenny, I gave it to her to look after and she never let me down.

'One day her husband died out at the villa. So I did my best by hook or by crook to get to her. After all, you know, a friend in need is a friend indeed.

'Luckily the master had gone off to Capua to look after some odds and ends. I seized my chance and I talked a guest of ours into walking with me as far as the fifth milestone. He was a soldier as it happened, and as brave as hell. About cock-crow we shag off, and the moon was shining like noon-time. We get to where the tombs are and my chap starts making for the grave-stones, while I, singing away, keep going and start counting the stars. Then just as I looked back at my mate, he stripped off and laid all his clothes by the side of the road. My heart was in my mouth, I stood there like a corpse. Anyway, he pissed a ring round his clothes and suddenly turned into a wolf. Don't think I'm joking, I wouldn't tell a lie about this for a fortune. However, as I began to say, after he turned into a wolf, he started howling and rushed off into the woods.

'At first I didn't know where I was, then I went up to collect his clothes – but they'd turned to stone. If ever a man was dead with fright, it was me. But I pulled out my sword, and I fairly slaughtered the early morning shadows till I arrived at my girl's villa.

'I got into the house and I practically gasped my last, the sweat was pouring down my crotch, my eyes were blank and staring – I could hardly get over it. It came as a surprise to my poor Melissa to find I'd walked over so late.

'"If you'd come a bit earlier," she said, "at least you could've helped us. A wolf got into the grounds and tore into all the livestock – it was like a bloody shambles. But he didn't have the last laugh, even though he got away. Our slave here put a spear right through his neck."

'I couldn't close my eyes again after I heard this. But when it was broad daylight I rushed off home like the innkeeper after the robbery. And when I came to the spot where his clothes had turned to stone, I found nothing but bloodstains. However, when I got home, my soldier friend was lying in bed like a great ox with the doctor seeing to his neck. I realized he was a werewolf and afterwards I couldn't have taken a bite of bread in his company, not if you killed me for it. If some people think differently about this, that's up to them. But me – if I'm telling a lie may all your guardian spirits damn me!'

Everyone was struck with amazement.

'I wouldn't disbelieve a word,' said Trimalchio. 'Honestly, the way my hair stood on end – because I know Niceros doesn't go in for jokes. He's really reliable and never exaggerates.

'Now I'll tell you a horrible story myself. A real donkey on the roof! When I was still in long hair (you see, I led a very soft life from my boyhood) the master's pet slave died. He was a pearl, honest to god, a beautiful boy, and one of the best. Well, his poor mother was crying over him and the rest of us were deep in depression, when the witches suddenly started howling – you'd think it was a dog after a hare.

'At that time we had a Cappadocian chap, tall and a very brave old thing, quite the strong man – he could lift an angry ox. This fellow rushed outside with a drawn sword, first wrapping his left hand up very carefully, and he stabbed one of the women right through the middle, just about here – may no harm come to where I'm touching! We heard a groan but – naturally I'm not lying – we didn't see the things themselves. Our big fellow, however, once he was back inside, threw himself on his bed. His whole body was black and blue, as though he'd been whipped. The evil hand, you see, had been put on him.

'We closed the door and went back to what we had to do, but as the mother puts her arms round her son's body, she touches it and finds it's only a handful of straw. It had no heart, no inside, no anything. Of course the witches had already stolen the boy and put a straw baby in its place.

'I put it to you, you can't get away from it – there are such things as women with special powers and midnight hags that can turn everything upside down. But that great tall fellow of ours never got his colour back after what happened. In fact, not many days later, he went crazy and died.'

Equally thrilled and convinced, we kissed the table and asked the midnight hags to stay at home till we got back from dinner.

By this time, to tell the truth, there seemed to be more lights burning and the whole dining-room seemed different, when Trimalchio said:

'What about you, Plocamus, haven't you a story to entertain us with. You used to have a fine voice for giving recitations with a nice swing and putting songs over – ah me, the good old days are gone.'

'Well,' said Plocamus, 'my galloping days finished after I got gout. Besides, when I was really young I nearly got consumption through singing. How about my dancing? How about my recitations? How about my barber's shop act? When was there anybody so good apart from Apelles himself?'

Putting his hand to his mouth he let out some sort of obscene whistle which he afterwards insisted was Greek.

Trimalchio, after giving us his own imitation of a fanfare of trumpets, looked round for his little pet, whom he called Croesus. The boy, however, a bleary-eyed creature with absolutely filthy teeth, was busy wrapping a green cloth round a disgustingly fat black puppy. He put half a loaf on the couch and was cramming it down the animal's throat while it kept vomiting it back. This business reminded Trimalchio to send out for Scylax, 'protector of the house and the household'.

A hound of enormous size was immediately led in on a chain. A kick from the hall-porter reminded him to lie down and he stretched himself out in front of the table. Trimalchio threw him a piece of white bread, remarking:

'Nobody in the house is more devoted to me.'

The boy, however, annoyed by such a lavish tribute to Scylax, put his own little pup on the floor and encouraged her to hurry up and start a fight. Scylax, naturally following his canine instincts, filled the dining-room with a most unpleasant barking and almost tore Croesus' Pearl to pieces.

Nor was the trouble limited to the dog-fight. A lampstand was upset on the table as well and not only smashed all the glass but spilled hot oil over some of the guests.

Not wanting to seem disturbed by the damage, Trimalchio gave the boy a kiss and told him to climb on his back. The lad climbed on his mount without hesitation, and slapping his shoulder blades with the flat of his hand, shouted amid roars of laughter:

'Big mouth, big mouth, how many fingers have I got up?'

So Trimalchio was calmed down for a while and gave instructions for a huge bowl of drink to be mixed and served to all the servants, who were sitting by our feet. He added the condition:

'If anyone won't take it, pour it over his head. Day's the time for business, now's the time for fun.'

This display of kindness was followed by some savouries, the very recollection of which really and truly makes me sick. Instead of thrushes, a fat capon was brought round for each of us, as well as goose-eggs in pastry hoods. Trimalchio surpassed himself to make us eat them; he described them as boneless chickens. In the middle of all this, a lictor knocked at the double doors and a drunken guest entered wearing white, followed by a large crowd of people. I was terrified by this lordly apparition and thought it was the chief magistrate arriving. So I tried to rise and get my bare feet on the floor. Agamemnon laughed at this panic and said:

'Get hold of yourself, you silly fool. This is Habinnas – Augustan College and monumental mason.'

Relieved by this information I resumed my position and watched Habinnas' entry with huge admiration. Being already drunk, he had his hands on his wife's shoulders; loaded with several garlands, oil pouring down his forehead and into his eyes, he settled himself into the praetor's place of honour and immediately demanded some wine and hot water. Trimalchio, delighted by these high spirits, demanded a larger cup for himself and asked how he had enjoyed it all.

'The only thing we missed,' replied Habinnas, 'was yourself – the apple of my eye was here. Still, it was damn good. Scissa was giving a ninth-day dinner in honour of a poor slave of hers she'd freed on his death-bed. And I think she'll have a pretty penny to pay with the five per cent liberation tax, because they reckon he was worth fifty thousand. Still, it was pleasant enough, even if we did have to pour half our drinks over his wretched bones.'

'Well,' said Trimalchio, 'what did you have for dinner?'

'I'll tell you if I can – I've such a good memory that I often forget my own name. For the first course we had a pig crowned with sausages and served with blood-puddings and very nicely done giblets, and of course beetroot and pure wholemeal bread – which I prefer to white myself: it's very strengthening and I don't regret it when I do my business. The next course was cold tart and a concoction of first-class Spanish wine poured over hot honey. I didn't eat anything at all of the actual tart, but I got stuck into the honey. Scattered round were chickpeas, lupines, a choice of nuts and an apple apiece – though I took two. And look, I've got them tied up in a napkin, because if I don't take something in the way of a present to my little slave, I'll have a row on my hands.

'Oh yes, my good lady reminds me. We had a hunk of

bear-meat set before us, which Scintilla was foolish enough to try, and she practically spewed up her guts; but I ate more than a pound of it, as it tasted like real wild-boar. And I say if bears can eat us poor people, it's all the more reason why us poor people should eat bears.

'To finish up with, we had some cheese basted with new wine, snails all round, chitterlings, plates of liver, eggs in pastry hoods, turnips, mustard, and then, wait a minute, little tunny fish! There were pickled cumin seeds too, passed round in a bowl, and some people were that bad-mannered they took three handfuls. You see, we sent the ham away.

'But tell me something, Gaius, now I ask – why isn't Fortunata at the table?'

'You know her,' replied Trimalchio, 'unless she's put the silver away and shared out the leftovers among the slaves, she won't put a drop of water to her mouth.'

'All the same,' retorted Habinnas, 'unless she sits down, I'm shagging off.'

And he was starting to get up, when at a given signal all the servants shouted '*Fortunata*' four or more times. So in she came with her skirt tucked up under a yellow sash to show her cerise petticoat underneath, as well as her twisted anklets and gold-embroidered slippers. Wiping her hands on a handkerchief which she carried round her neck, she took her place on the couch where Habinnas' wife was reclining. She kissed her. 'Is it really you?' she said, clapping her hands together.

It soon got to the point where Fortunata took the bracelets from her great fat arms and showed them to the admiring Scintilla. In the end she even undid her anklets and her gold hair net, which she said was pure gold. Trimalchio noticed this and had it all brought to him and commented:

'A woman's chains, you see. This is the way us poor fools get robbed. She must have six and a half pounds on her. Still, I've got a bracelet myself, made up from one-tenth per cent to Mercury – and it weighs not an ounce less than ten pounds.'

Finally, for fear he looked like a liar, he even had some scales brought in and had them passed round to test the weight.

Scintilla was no better. From round her neck she took a little gold locket, which she called her 'lucky box'. From it she extracted two earrings and in her turn gave them to Fortunata to look at.

'A present from my good husband,' she said, 'and no one has a finer set.'

'Hey!' said Habinnas. 'You cleaned me out to buy you a glass bean. Honestly, if I had a daughter, I'd cut her little ears off. If there weren't any women, everything would be dirt cheap. As it is, we've got to drink cold water and piss it out hot.'

Meanwhile, the women giggled tipsily between themselves and kissed each other drunkenly, one crying up her merits as a housewife, the other crying about her husband's demerits and boy-friends. While they had their heads together like this, Habinnas rose stealthily and taking Fortunata's feet, flung them up over the couch.

'Oh, oh!' she shrieked, as her underskirt wandered up over her knees. So she settled herself in Scintilla's lap and hid her burning red face in her handkerchief.

Then came an interval, after which Trimalchio called for dessert. Slaves removed all the tables and brought in others. They scattered sawdust tinted with saffron and vermilion, and something I had never seen before – powdered mica. Trimalchio said at once:

'I could make you just settle for this. There's dessert for you! The first tables've deserted. However, if you people have anything nice, bring it on!'

Meanwhile a slave from Alexandria, who was taking round the hot water, started imitating a nightingale, only for Trimalchio to shout: 'Change your tune!'

More entertainment! A slave sitting by Habinnas' feet, prompted, I suppose, by his master, suddenly burst out in a sing-song voice:

'Meantime Aeneas was in mid-ocean with his fleet.'

No more cutting sound ever pierced my eardrums. Apart from his barbarous meandering up and down the scale, he mixed in Atellan verses, so that Virgil actually grated on me for the first time in my life. When he did finally stop through exhaustion, Habinnas said:

'He's never had any real training. I just had him taught by sending him along to peddlers on the street corner. He's no one to equal him if he wants to imitate mule-drivers or hawkers. He's terribly clever, really. He's a cobbler, a cook, a confectioner – a man that can turn his hand to anything. But he's got two faults; if he didn't have them, he'd be one in a million – he's circumcised and he snores. I don't mind him being cross-eyed – so is Venus. That's why he's never quiet and his eyes are hardly ever still. I got him for three hundred denarii.'

Scintilla interrupted him: 'Of course, you're not telling them all the tricks that wretch gets up to. He's a pimp – but I'll make sure he gets branded for it.'

Trimalchio laughed: 'I know a Cappadocian when I see one. He's not slow in looking after himself and, by heaven, I admire him for it. You can't take it with you.

'Now, Scintilla, don't be jealous. Believe me, we know all about you women too. As sure as I stand here, I used to bang the mistress so much that even the old boy suspected; so he sent me off to look after his farms. But I'd better save my breath to cool my porridge.'

As though he'd been complimented the wretched slave took out an earthenware lamp from his pocket and for more than half an hour gave imitations of trumpet-players, while Habinnas hummed an accompaniment, pressing down his lower lip with his hand. Finally coming right into the middle, he did a flute-player with some broken reeds, then he dressed up in a greatcoat and whip and did the Life of the Muleteer, till Habinnas called him over, kissed him, and gave him a drink:

'Better and better, Massa!' he said. 'I'll give you a pair of boots.'

There would have been no end to all these trials if an extra course had not arrived – pastry thrushes stuffed with raisins and nuts. After them came quinces with thorns stuck in them to look like sea urchins. All this would have been all right, but there was a far more horrible dish that made us prefer even dying of hunger. When it was put on the table, looking

to us like a fat goose surrounded by fish and all sorts of
game, Trimalchio said:

'Whatever you see here, friends, is made from one kind of
stuff.'

I, of course, being very cautious by nature, spotted immediately what it was and glancing at Agamemnon, I said:

'I'll be surprised if it isn't all made of wax, or any rate
mud. I've seen that sort of imitation food produced at the
Saturnalia in Rome.'

I hadn't quite finished what I was saying when Trimalchio
said:

'As sure as I hope to expand – my investments of course,
not my waist-line – my chef made it all from pork. There
couldn't be a more valuable man to have. Say the word and
he'll produce a fish out of a sow's belly, a pigeon out of the
lard, a turtle dove out of the ham, and fowl out of the
knuckle. So he's been given a nice name I thought of
myself – he's called Daedalus. And seeing he's a clever lad,
I brought him some carvers of Styrian steel as a present from
Rome.'

He immediately had them brought in and gazed at them
with admiration. He even allowed us to test the point on our
cheeks.

All of a sudden in came two slaves, apparently having had
a quarrel at the well; at any rate they still had water jugs on
their shoulders. But while Trimalchio was giving his decision
about their respective cases, neither of them paid any atten-
tion to his verdict: instead they broke each other's jugs with
their sticks. Staggered by their drunken insolence, we
couldn't take our eyes away from the fight till we noticed

oysters and scallops sliding out of the jugs, which a boy collected and carried round on a dish. The ingenious chef was equal to these elegant refinements – he brought in snails on a silver gridiron, singing all the time in a high grating voice.

I blush to say what happened next. Boys with their hair down their backs came round with perfumed cream in a silver bowl and rubbed it on our feet as we lay there, but first they wrapped our legs and ankles in wreaths of flowers. Some of the same stuff was dropped into the decanter and the lamp.

Fortunata was now wanting to dance, and Scintilla was doing more clapping than talking, when Trimalchio said:

'Philargyrus – even though you are such a terrible fan of the Greens – you have my permission to join us. And tell your dear Menophila to sit down as well.'

Need I say more? We were almost thrown out of our places, so completely did the household fill the dining-room. I even noticed that the chef, the one who had produced the goose out of pork, was actually given a place above me, and he was reeking of pickles and sauce. And he wasn't satisfied with just having a place, but he had to start straight off on an imitation of the tragedian Ephesus, and then challenge his master to bet against the Greens winning at the next races.

Trimalchio became expansive after this argument.

'My dear people,' he said, 'slaves are human beings too. They drink the same milk as anybody else, even though luck's been agin 'em. Still, if nothing happens to me, they'll have their taste of freedom soon. In fact, I'm setting them all free in my will. I'm giving Philargyrus a farm, what's more, and the woman he lives with. As for Cario, I'm leaving him a block of flats, his five per cent manumission tax, and a bed with all the trimmings. I'm making Fortunata my heir, and I want all my friends to look after her.

'The reason I'm telling everyone all this is so my household will love me now as much as if I was dead.'

Everyone began thanking his lordship for his kindness, when he became very serious and had a copy of his will brought in. Amid the sobs of his household he read out the whole thing from beginning to end.

Then looking at Habinnas, he said:

'What have you to say, my dear old friend? Are you building my monument the way I told you? I particularly want you to keep a place at the foot of my statue and put a picture of my pup there, as well as paintings of wreaths, scent-bottles, and all the contests of Petraites, and thanks to you I'll be able to live on after I'm dead. And another thing! See that it's a hundred feet facing the road and two hundred back into the field. I want all the various sorts of fruit round my ashes and lots and lots of vines. After all, it's a big mistake to have nice houses just for when you're alive and not worry about the one we have to live in for much longer. And that's why I want this written up before anything else:

THIS MONUMENT DOES NOT GO TO THE HEIR

'But I'll make sure in my will that I don't get done down once I'm dead. I'll put one of my freedmen in charge of my tomb to look after it and not let people run up and shit on my monument. I'd like you to put some ships there too, sailing under full canvas, and me sitting on a high platform in my robes of office, wearing five gold rings and pouring out a bagful of money for the people. You know I gave them all a dinner and two denarii apiece. Let's have in a banqueting hall as well, if you think it's a good idea, and show the whole town having a good time. Put up a statue of Fortunata on my right, holding a dove, and have her leading her little dog tied to her belt – and my little lad as well, and big wine-jars tightly sealed up so the wine won't spill. And perhaps you could carve me a broken one and a boy crying over it. A clock in the middle, so that anybody who looks at the time, like it or not, has got to read my name. As for the inscription now, take a good look and see if this seems suitable enough:

HERE SLEEPS
GAIUS POMPEIUS TRIMALCHIO
MAECENATIANUS
ELECTED TO THE AUGUSTAN COLLEGE IN HIS ABSENCE
HE COULD HAVE BEEN ON EVERY BOARD IN ROME
BUT HE REFUSED
GOD-FEARING BRAVE AND TRUE
A SELF-MADE MAN
HE LEFT AN ESTATE OF 30,000,000
AND HE NEVER HEARD A PHILOSOPHER
FAREWELL
AND YOU FARE WELL, TRIMALCHIO'

As he finished Trimalchio burst into tears. Fortunata was in tears, Habinnas was in tears, in the end the whole household filled the dining-room with their wailing, like people at a funeral. In fact, I'd even begun crying myself, when Trimalchio said:

'Well, since we know we've got to die, why don't we live a little. I want to see you enjoying yourselves. Let's jump into a bath – you won't be sorry, damn me! It's as hot as a furnace.'

'Hear! Hear!' said Habinnas. 'Turning one day into two – nothing I like better.' He got up in his bare feet and began to follow Trimalchio on his merry way.

I looked at Ascyltus. 'What do you think?' I said. 'Now me, if I see a bath, I'll die on the spot.'

'Let's say yes,' he suggested, 'and while they're going for their bath, we can slip out in the crowd.'

This seemed a good idea, so Giton led us through the portico till we reached the door, where the hound chained there greeted us with such a noise that Ascyltus actually fell into the fishpond. Not only that, as I was drunk too, when I tried to help the struggling Ascyltus I was dragged into the same watery trap. However, the hall-porter saved us and by his intervention pacified the dog and dragged us trembling to dry land. Giton had already bought off the beast in a most ingenious way. He had scattered whatever he had got from us at dinner in front of the barking hound, and distracted by the food, it had choked down its fury.

Nevertheless, when, shivering and wet, we asked the hall-porter to let us out through the front door, he said: 'You're wrong if you think you can leave through the door you came in. No guest has ever been let out through the same door. They come in one way and go out another.'

What could we do after this piece of bad luck, shut up in this modern labyrinth and now beginning to regret that bath? We asked him to please show us the way to the bath-hall, and, throwing off our clothes, which Giton began drying at the door, we went in. There stood Trimalchio, and not even there could we get away from his filthy ostentation. He told us there was nothing better than a private bath, and that there had once been a bakery on that very spot. Then he sat down as though tired, and being tempted by the acoustics of the bath, with his drunken mouth gaping at the ceiling, he began murdering some songs by Menecrates – or so we were told by those who understood his words.